THE ONE AND ONLY $ COMMON SENSE S

Check It Out

The Book About Banking

by Neale S. Godfrey

Illustrated by Randy Verougstraete

Modern Curriculum Press
Parsippany, New Jersey

To the children of the world:
The future is yours. We nurture you, we teach you,
we love you because every child is our child.

Editorial assistance provided by Pubworks, Inc.
Design: Rosanne Guarara

All photographs by Silver Burdett Ginn (SBG) unless otherwise noted.

8: Michael Rosenfeld/Tony Stone Images. 11: Michael Newman/PhotoEdit. 14: Vic Bider/Tony Stone Images. 32: Reuters/Corbis-Bettmann.

Modern Curriculum Press
An Imprint of Pearson Learning
299 Jefferson Road
Parsippany, NJ 07054

ISBN 0-7652-1767-8

2 3 4 5 6 7 8 9 10 CA 06 05 04 03 02 01 00

A Note to Kids

So, you're making some money. You've got an allowance or a job, or maybe you've just received some money as a gift. What are you going to do with it? You could keep it in a shoe box at home, or maybe under your mattress. But that doesn't seem very safe. How about a bank? You may think that a bank is a great idea, but you're not so sure why.

Well, welcome to *Check It Out: The Book About Banking*. This book will help you learn about banks: how they work, and the services they provide. When it comes to banking, there are a lot of options: savings accounts, checking accounts, loans, debit cards, and interest rates. Where you put your money and how you manage it are up to you. *Check It Out: The Book About Banking* will help you untangle this mess of choices, and show you how to start off on the right foot! You'll unravel the mysteries of credit cards and discover that banking and managing your credit are things you *can* handle.

Saving, spending wisely, sharing, and planning for the future are important skills that you will need as you grow older. Money itself is neither good nor bad. It is what is done with money that counts. *Check It Out: The Book About Banking* will help you discover how interesting banking can be and how worthwhile the knowledge is!

Neale S. Godfrey

Contents

Chapter 1

All About Banks

It's your **money**.
You **make** it.
You **spend** it.
You **save** it.

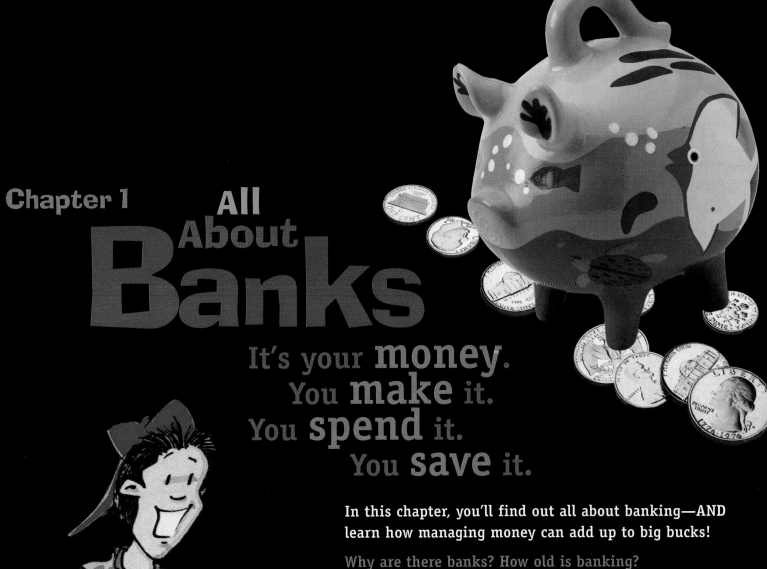

In this chapter, you'll find out all about banking—AND learn how managing money can add up to big bucks!

Why are there banks? How old is banking?
How do I know if my money is safe in a bank?
How do banks make money?
What are some alternatives to banks?

These are just a few of the questions you'll find answers to. By the end of this chapter, you'll have a better understanding of the statement *You can bank on it!*

Bank Notes, Facts,

Banking: It's an Old Story

Banking is as old as money itself, dating back thousands of years. In ancient times, temples were the safest places to store precious metals. No one would steal from a temple for fear of making the gods angry. So temples became the first **banks**. There are records that date back 2,000 years, showing how much precious metal individuals had deposited in temples. Some temples even exchanged foreign coins and made **loans**, which let people borrow money with the promise to pay it back.

In ancient Greece, each city had its own coins. Traveling merchants paid money-changers a fee to exchange coins from one city for those from another. Money-changers also exchanged coins for gold or silver. The services money changers provided encouraged trade between different cities and foreign countries. Money-changers became the first bankers. Later in history, goldsmiths acted as bankers by keeping people's valuable possessions in their vaults.

A Matter of Fact

Early Italian bankers often conducted their business on street benches. The English word *bank* comes from the Italian word *banca*, which means "bench."

The first U.S. bank was established in 1791.

Wow! That was even before my great-great-great-grandmother was born!

2

Word Bank

bank *a business that keeps money for customers, makes loans, and provides other money-related services*

loan *a sum of money borrowed for a certain amount of time*

and Figures

Banks: Minding Your—and Their—Own Business!

Besides being a safe place to keep money, a bank is also a business. Like any other business, a bank needs to make a **profit**. Profit is the money left after a business pays its expenses. Banks make money by charging their customers for the services they provide.

Banks also make money by lending money. When you **deposit** your money in a bank, you are letting the bank use it. The bank combines your money with other depositors' money to make loans. In return for using your money, the bank pays you **interest**. The bank can then lend your money to someone who wants to borrow it. The borrower has to pay interest to the bank. But the borrower pays the bank more interest than the bank pays you. So the bank makes a profit by being the go-between—just like the money-changers in the old days.

Interest on loan 10%

Interest on savings 5%

Word Bank

profit *the money left over after expenses are paid*

deposit *the money put in a bank account*

interest *the money you pay to borrow money, or the money a bank pays you for using your money*

Simply Interest-ing!

How does interest work? Suppose you put $100 in the bank and the bank agrees to pay you 5% interest per year. This means that the bank will pay you 5¢ per dollar every year. At the end of the first year, you will have earned $5. How much money would you have? What if you put $1,000 in the bank for one year at the same interest rate?

3

The Golden Rules

- Banks must insure their customers' deposits.
- Banks must keep a percentage of their deposits in a Federal Reserve bank.
- Banks must tell customers the interest rate on a loan.
- All agreements that bank customers sign must be written in plain English so that the customer understands exactly what it is he or she is signing.
- Banks may not make loans unless they are sure the loans will be repaid.
- Banks may not discriminate against anyone on account of age, sex, religion, race, or ethnic background.

The Loan Ranger

Are banks allowed to lend all of their money? No, of course not! The Federal Reserve System, the central bank of the United States, makes sure banks take good care of your money. The "Fed" requires that banks keep a certain percentage of their deposits on hand or in a Federal Reserve bank. That way, when people want their money back, they can get it.

A Penny for Your Thoughts

Government laws limit the interest that banks may charge for loans. What do you think would happen if there were no such laws? Do you think all banks charge the same rates? Are these laws good for the customer?

Keeping Track of
Business

How do banks keep track of everyone's money? By keeping accurate records of every **transaction** in each customer's account. Customers fill out slips of paper for every deposit or **withdrawal**. They get a receipt from the bank, which is proof of the transaction. Most banks provide customers with a **bank statement**, a summary of the transactions that occurred during the month. The bank statement also shows the **balance**, the amount remaining in the account after each transaction.

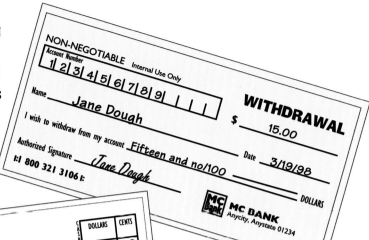

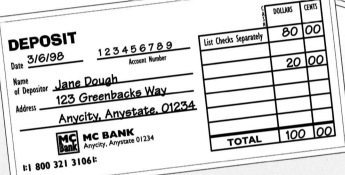

Word Bank

transaction *any business done with the bank, such as a deposit or withdrawal*

withdrawal *the removal of money from a bank account*

bank statement *a monthly summary of a customer's transactions*

balance *the amount of money in a bank account*

SAVINGS ACCOUNT STATEMENT

Account Number: 123456789
Date of Statement: April 1, 1998
Closing Balance: $463.00

Date	Description	Debit	Credit	Balance
3/1	Opening Balance			
3/6	Deposit		$100.00	$328.00
3/19	Withdrawal	$15.00		$428.00
3/27	Deposit		$50.00	$413.00
				$463.00

Big Banks, Little

Bank on It!

As you've probably noticed, banks are found in many different places, from main streets to supermarkets. There are banks in every country in the world. Did you know, though, that there are different kinds of banks? There are commercial banks, savings banks, and credit unions. Although banks generally serve either businesses or individuals, all banks offer similar services.

Commercial Banks Commercial banks were originally created to meet the needs of businesses. Today, most banks are commercial banks. They deal with individuals and with businesses. Commercial banks offer a variety of services. These services include checking accounts, savings accounts, and loans.

Savings Banks Savings banks were founded to give working people a place to save their money. Today, these banks are similar to commercial banks except that they mostly offer savings accounts and loans, so people can buy homes. Loans for buying homes are called **mortgages**.

Credit Unions Credit unions were started to help people borrow money. A group of people who had a common bond—for example, workers in a steel mill—pooled their savings. Like commercial banks, credit unions offer checking accounts, savings accounts, and loans. Unlike commercial banks, credit unions are nonprofit. This means that any profits the credit union makes are shared with the members.

> What's a savings account? What's a checking account? Just keep reading to find out!

A Matter of Fact

Did you ever have a piggy bank? Did you know its name has nothing to do with the animal? The piggy bank got its name from a kind of clay called *pygg*. Years ago, people stored their money in clay jars for safekeeping. These jars were called pygg banks. Eventually, the name changed to "piggy bank," and people actually began making them in the shape of a pig.

Banks, Piggy Banks

The **Banks'** Bank

As you read before, the Federal Reserve is the central bank of the United States. Most countries have a central bank to help regulate money. The Fed is not a typical bank, though. You can't deposit money there—but banks can. The Fed controls the money supply for the entire country. It does this by lending money to banks when they need it, but controlling the amount of money it lends.

Just as banks charge interest to customers who borrow money, the Fed charges interest to banks for borrowing money. But just as you wouldn't want to borrow money when interest rates are high, neither do banks. When the interest rate is high, banks borrow less money. That means there is less money in **circulation**—that is, there is less money available to use. It's up to the Fed to make sure that the total amount of money in circulation in the country is just right—not too much, not too little.

The Federal Reserve System was created by an act of Congress in 1913.

Wow! That's some act!

A Penny for Your Thoughts

Sometimes, banks need extra money to meet their customers' demands. They get this cash from their regional Federal Reserve Bank. At what times of year do you think bank customers withdraw large sums of money?

Banking—It's a Career

It takes a lot of people to run a bank. Each job requires different responsibilities and different levels of education. Some examples are listed below.

High School Degree

- A **teller** withdraws and deposits money for customers.
- A **security officer** maintains safety at the bank.
- A **proof machine operator** runs equipment at the bank and subtracts money from bank accounts.

College or Graduate Degree

- A **loan officer** arranges loans to businesses and individuals.
- An **accountant** keeps the financial records for a bank.
- A **lawyer** attends to a bank's legal matters.

Word Bank

mortgage *a loan given to pay for a house or building*

circulation *money that is available for use*

7

At Your Service

Banks earn money by investing their own money and by charging customers money, or **fees**, for different bank services. Like other businesses, banks are always looking for new customers. More customers mean more money for the bank. So banks offer services and conveniences they think will be attractive to consumers. These include special accounts and loans with low interest rates.

Safe and Sound

When you put money in a bank, you can be sure it is safe. Money is kept in steel vaults, which can only be opened by certain people, under very tight security. Did you know that bank vaults are fireproof?

But what happens if your bank is robbed or just goes out of business? A government agency called the FDIC, or Federal Deposit Insurance Corporation, will give you your money. By federal law, banks must insure customer accounts up to $100,000 with the FDIC.

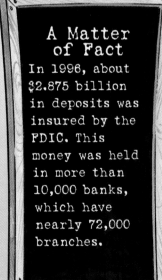

A Matter of Fact

In 1996, about $2.875 billion in deposits was insured by the FDIC. This money was held in more than 10,000 banks, which have nearly 72,000 branches.

Personal Treasures

If banks are such safe places to keep your money, why not keep other valuable items there, too? Well, you can! Many banks allow you to keep things like jewelry or important papers in a **safe-deposit box** at the bank. For a yearly fee, the bank will give you your own fireproof box and key. The bank keeps your safe-deposit box in a huge walk-in vault. Most safe-deposit boxes are about the same size as a shoe box. What would *you* put in a safe-deposit box?

safe-deposit boxes

Word Bank

fee *money charged for a service*

safe-deposit box *a place to keep special items in a bank*

8

Count on Them!

So Where's the Money?

Here's an interesting fact: Most of the money on deposit in the bank isn't really there—it's just a computer entry! This is because banks only need to keep a small amount of deposits in cash. What happens if a lot of people want to withdraw large sums of money from the bank at the same time? The bank orders cash from its Federal Reserve bank.

Look! No Paycheck!

When do you think a lot of people go to the bank? If you guessed on "payday," you're probably right! Many people receive a **check** from their company when they are paid. A check is a piece of paper that tells the bank to pay the person named on the check the amount of money specified. Did you know that many companies now offer **direct deposit** of paychecks? With this service, the company electronically deposits an employee's paycheck into his or her bank account. Sometime in the future, people won't have to use cash or checks at all!

A Penny for Your Thoughts

Some banks charge a fee for PC banking. Others encourage customers to try PC banking by making it available free of charge. How do you think PC banking benefits the bank or the customer?

Home-Based Banking

So you don't want to walk to the bank? If you have a personal computer (PC), and a modem (which lets your computer send messages over a phone line), you may not have to. **PC banking** lets you manage your money from home by linking your computer directly to your bank's computer. You can check your account balance, transfer money from one account to another, open new accounts—even pay bills electronically! You can do almost anything you can do at the bank, except make cash deposits or withdrawals.

Word Bank

check *a written order to a bank to pay a specified amount of money to a specified person or company, from money on deposit with the bank*

direct deposit *electronic deposit of checks in the bank*

PC banking *using a home or office computer to carry out bank transactions*

Don't tell anyone your PIN! Keep it a secret.

A Bank in Your Pocket—
The ATM Card

Do you have cash in your bank account that you need? Is the bank closed? Don't worry. It's not a problem if you have access to an **automated-teller machine (ATM)**. An ATM takes the place of human tellers. Unlike people, though, ATMs work 24 hours a day, 7 days a week, without a break. This means that you can use an ATM whenever it's convenient for you. You'll find ATMs in bank lobbies and in other accessible places around town.

Do you know what happens when you put your **ATM card** in the ATM? When your card is inserted, you are asked to enter a "secret code." This is your **personal identification number (PIN)**. If the ATM does not recognize your PIN, you will not be able to carry out any transactions at the ATM.

A Matter of Fact
Transactions at an ATM cost a bank a lot less than teller transactions at the bank. Because of this, some banks now charge a fee to use a teller!

If you lose your ATM card, let the bank know right away.

Always know how much is in your account. Keep track of all transactions you make, including any charges or fees.

Word Bank

automated-teller machine (ATM) *a machine that performs most of the banking operations that a human teller can*

ATM card *a bank card that allows customers to use an ATM machine*

personal identification number (PIN) *a code that activates an ATM card*

Now I'm Here,
What Can I Do?

What kinds of banking can you do at an ATM? You can make deposits and withdrawals. You can check your account balance. You can transfer money between accounts. The machine will give you a receipt for the transaction just made and tell you your new balance. Be careful! Some banks charge a fee each time you use an ATM.

No Cash?
No Problem!

Suppose you want to make a purchase. You don't have enough cash with you, but you do have the money in your checking account. You could use a bank **debit card**. A debit is money subtracted from an account. When you use your debit card, money is taken from your checking account to pay for something. You can also use a debit card at an ATM for your banking transactions, just as you would an ATM card. Sometimes an ATM card can be used as a debit card, too!

It's Not Magic—
How a Debit Card Works

When you use your debit card at a store, the shopkeeper slides your card through the card-reading machine. The machine contacts your bank electronically to make sure there's enough money in your checking account to pay for your purchase. If you do have enough money, that amount is automatically subtracted from your account and sent to the store's account to pay for your purchase.

Suppose you have $20.00 in your checking account and you want to buy something with your debit card that costs $18.50. That amount will be subtracted from your checking account, leaving you with a balance of $1.50. What if you only had $15.00 in your checking account? Then the store will not let you use your debit card to make that purchase. How could you still make the purchase?

Word Bank

debit card *a bank card that allows a person to withdraw money electronically from a checking account*

Print VERSATEL® Statements at this ATM Get Cash • Make Deposits

Get a Detailed Statement Here!

Not Everyone Banks

Cash and Carry

Banks offer a lot of services, but these services cost money. Some banks charge customers a monthly service fee for having a checking account. Other banks charge fees to customers who do not maintain a **minimum balance** in their accounts. That means that customers must keep a certain amount of money in the account. Sometimes the minimum balance may be thousands of dollars!

UNITED STATES POSTAL MONEY ORDER

15-800
000

***5*00

6666270 3797 970916 079450 ***5*00

U.S. DOLLARS AND CENTS

SERIAL NUMBER

YEAR, MONTH, DAY

CHECKWRITER IMPRINT AREA

POST OFFICE

PAY TO   Fast Photo

FROM   Jane Dough

ADDRESS   9863 West Street
Anycity, Anystate 01234

ADDRESS   123 Greenbacks Way
Anycity, Anystate 01234

C.O.D. NO. OR USED FOR   School Picture Reprint

NEGOTIABLE ONLY IN THE U.S. AND POSSESSIONS

6666270 3797

I:00000800 2I:

Some people can't afford or don't need personal checking accounts. Suppose you didn't have a checking account, but you needed to pay some bills. What would you do? You could pay your bills with cash. But what if you needed to mail your payments? If your mail was lost or stolen, your cash would be gone! Instead, you could buy a **money order** at a bank or post office for a small fee. Like a check, a money order can only be cashed by the person whose name is on it. Unlike a check, money orders can be cashed anywhere they are sold.

Cashing In

Many people in the United States don't use banks at all. Some people can't afford, or choose not to pay, banking fees. Others may have work that keeps them moving from place to place. Without a bank account, it's not easy to **cash** a check—that is, to exchange the check for cash. What's the answer? A check-cashing business.

In exchange for cashing a check, the check-cashing business charges a fee, usually a portion of the dollar amount of the check. So check-cashing businesses provide instant cash to people without bank accounts. Without this service, many people could not cash their checks.

Word Bank

minimum balance *a fixed amount of money required in a customer's account to avoid paying bank fees*

money order *a written order, or check, that a certain sum of money be paid to a certain person or business*

cash *bills and coins, or to give or get cash for, as in to cash a check*

Fast Cash

Where can you go to borrow money if you need money right away? Borrowing money from a bank takes time. You need to apply for a loan and then wait for approval from the bank. What else can you do? One answer is to go to a **pawnshop**. Pawnshops are stores where you can leave something of value, such as a guitar or a camera, in exchange for a loan. The **pawnbroker**, who owns the pawnshop, will give you the money, along with a pawn ticket. With the ticket, property can be reclaimed for the amount of the loan, plus interest. However, there is a time limit to repay the loan. If the loan is not repaid, the pawnbroker keeps your property.

On Borrowed Time

A pawnshop loan can benefit both parties. The person needing money gets the money and the chance to "buy back" his or her property at a later date. The pawnbroker has something that is worth more than the cash loan just made. If the owner doesn't claim the property, the pawnbroker can sell the property for more than he or she paid for it. Today, there are fewer pawnshops than there used to be. That's because many people now have other means to pay for things when cash is scarce. You'll learn about those later on.

Word Bank

pawnshop *a place to leave an item of value in exchange for a loan*

pawnbroker *a person who lends money at a specified interest rate to people who leave items as security*

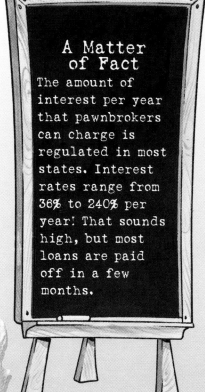

A Matter of Fact
The amount of interest per year that pawnbrokers can charge is regulated in most states. Interest rates range from 36% to 240% per year! That sounds high, but most loans are paid off in a few months.

Take Your Pick!

Count on It!

According to the Federal Reserve, there is about $525 billion in coins and bills in circulation today. How long would it take to count that amount if it takes 12 days without stopping to count to a million?

WOW, $525,000,000,000! That much money in one-dollar bills would be about 129,000 times taller than the Sears Tower, one of the tallest buildings in the world!

How does she know that?

Deposits and Withdrawals

Imagine your bank account was down to $75.00. You make 3 deposits of different amounts and 1 withdrawal. You now have $95.00. Yippee! How did you do it?

Break the Bank

Make your folks an offer they can't refuse. Tell them you'll walk the dog or take out the garbage each day for a month. Tell them they can pay you $20 for the month, or a penny the first day, two cents the second day, four cents the next day, eight cents the next day, and so on. Which offer should they accept?

14

Hint: It takes 233 stacked bills to equal one inch.
The Sears Tower is 1,454 feet tall.

Chapter 2

Savings Accounts and Checking Accounts

It's your **money.** Make a **home** for it!

Making money is hard work. But figuring out what to do with it can seem even harder. What do you do with it? Most people put money in the bank.

How do banks help you manage money?
What kind of a savings account is best for you?
How do you write checks and balance a checkbook?
What's the difference between bank checks, traveler's checks, cashier's checks, and bounced checks?

In this chapter you'll learn how to make money work for *you*.

Savings Accounts—

Save Now, Play Later

Do you like to spend money? Of course—who doesn't? But by now you've realized that it's important to save money for those little emergencies and the big and little things that you want. Sometimes you need to put off spending now in order to save for the future.

Stashing Your Cash

Where's the safest place to stash your cash? You can keep your money in a piggy bank, or you can hide it under your mattress. But if it just sits there, you are actually losing money! As you learned earlier, if you keep money in a savings account, the bank pays interest on your money. Your interest will earn interest, making you even more money!

Keeping your cash at home may seem like a smart move, but what happens if there's a fire? Or the money is lost or stolen?

Or if somebody like me sinks his teeth into it!

A Matter of Fact
During the gold rush days in the late 1800s, a rich woman put a lot of bills inside her wood-burning stove for safekeeping. She figured that burglars would never think to look there. But the woman forgot to tell her husband. One day her husband lit the stove—and their whole fortune went up in smoke!

It All Adds Up

Time to **Open an Account**

So you've decided to open a savings account. What do you do next? At the bank you'll probably fill out a signature card. To make sure you are who you say you are, you'll need identification, such as a birth certificate. You will also need to tell the bank your Social Security number. If you're under 18, a parent or guardian will need to help you open an account.

You Have to **Start Somewhere**

Sometimes the bank requires a certain amount of money, called a **minimum deposit**, to open an account. The minimum deposit may be as little as $5 or as much as $100 or more. It all depends on the bank you choose. Why do you think some banks want a minimum deposit? It's because it costs the bank money to hire the people to help you open a bank account, and then to manage it.

A Penny for Your Thoughts

Putting money in a bank is one way to save money. But you can save money by being careful, too. For example, you can turn off unneeded lights to lower your electric bill. You can make a meal at home instead of going out to eat. What are some other ways you can cut back spending to save money?

Word Bank

minimum deposit *the least amount of money required to open an account*

A Penny Saved
Is a Penny Earned

Did you know that there are three different kinds of savings accounts? Each type of account has different features and may pay a different amount of interest. Take a look!

Statement Savings Account A statement savings account is the most common bank savings account today. With this type of account, the bank sends you a statement once a month. The statement shows how much money you deposited or withdrew from your savings account, how much interest you earned, and how much money is in the account.

Passbook Accounts Do you always want to know how much money is in your account and what transactions have happened? Then a passbook account is for you. With this kind of account, every transaction you make, including interest your money has earned, is recorded in your passbook. Each time you make a deposit or a withdrawal, you give your passbook to the bank teller. The teller records each transaction in your passbook. Passbook accounts usually pay the same amount of interest as statement savings accounts.

ALWAYS VERIFY ENTRY BEFORE LEAVING WINDOW
THIS BOOK MUST BE PRESENTED FOR EVERY DEPOSIT OR WITHDRAWAL
IF LOST, NOTIFY BANK IMMEDIATELY

DATE	MEMO	DEPOSIT	WITHDRAWAL	INTEREST	BALANCE
					$350.00
01 03JUL		$350.00		.91	$350.91
02 01AUG					$250.91
03 18AUG			$100.00	.66	$251.57
04 01SEP					$336.57
05 26SEP		$ 85.00		.88	$337.45
06 01OCT					$437.45
07 25OCT		$100.00			

Certificate of Deposit (CD) What if you have some money that you don't plan to use for a while? You can buy a certificate of deposit. You deposit money, called **principal**, in the bank for a specific amount of time, such as six months or a year. You are not allowed to withdraw the money until the end of the time period—or else you pay a penalty! But because the bank knows how long it will have your money, it can lend it and not worry about when you will need it. This means you get more interest than you would in a regular savings account.

Wow! I've got a CD!

So do I!

CERTIFICATE OF DEPOSIT

CD PLAYER

Money Market Account What kind of savings account pays more interest than a regular savings account *and* lets you withdraw money by writing checks? A money market account! It's a great deal, but there are some limitations. You can usually write only a limited number of checks each month from this account. Also, money market accounts usually require a large minimum balance. Since you can withdraw your money at any time, banks pay a little less interest for this kind of account than for a CD.

Individual Retirement Account (IRA) Do you know what an IRA is? It's a savings account for your **retirement**. You are allowed to put a part of your income into an IRA each year. You do not have to pay taxes on this money until you take out the money. When you are retired and withdraw the money, the taxes you pay will be less.

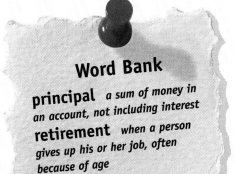

Word Bank

principal *a sum of money in an account, not including interest*

retirement *when a person gives up his or her job, often because of age*

Parents Can Bank on It

Sometimes, parents start saving for their children. Parents can open a special savings account called a trust account. Over the years, they can deposit money into it on a regular basis. When the children are old enough (usually 21 years old), they take over the account. By then the account has earned a lot of interest, because no money has been withdrawn! The children can use the trust account for big expenses like tuition or a mortgage. What are some reasons why parents might or might not open a trust account for their children?

> You'll check up on checks next.

A Matter of Fact Americans are really starting to save for retirement! In 1997, over $330 billion was stashed away in retirement accounts in U.S. banks. That's up from only $6.8 billion in 1977.

19

Checks and

Time for a Check Up

Many people choose to keep their money in two bank accounts: a savings account and a checking account. Do you know the difference? A checking account lets you keep your money in the bank, just like a savings account. But you usually have to be at least 18 years old to open a checking account. And the bank probably won't pay you interest on your money. Instead, it will let you write checks from that account. And checks can really come in handy!

Suppose you are buying a new bicycle for $150. That's a lot of money to carry around. So instead of carrying around the cash, you can write a check. A check tells your bank how much money to take from your bank account to give to someone else.

So all you need to carry is your checkbook—and maybe a pen! Don't write checks in pencil. The information could be erased or changed. Paying bills by check is a good idea. Do you know why? One reason is that a check is proof of payment.

This is the **date** you are writing the check.

This is the **amount** in numerals.

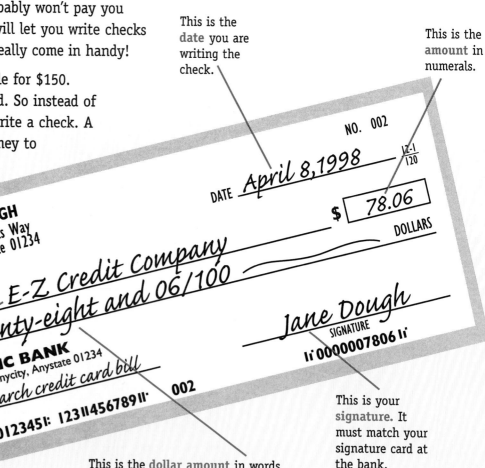

NO. 002

$\frac{12-1}{120}$

DATE _April 8, 1998_

$ _78.06_

JANE DOUGH
123 Greenbacks Way
Anycity, Anystate 01234

DOLLARS

PAY TO THE ORDER OF _E-Z Credit Company_

seventy-eight and 06/100

Jane Dough

SIGNATURE

MC BANK
Anycity, Anystate 01234

FOR _March credit card bill_   002

I:000012345I: 123II456789II·

Ii·0000007806 Ii·

This is the **name** of the person or company you want to pay.

This is the **dollar amount** in words and the cents in numerals. Always draw a line to fill the whole space. This prevents anyone from adding anything to your amount.

This is your **signature**. It must match your signature card at the bank.

Balances

Keeping Tabs on Your Checks

So, you've opened up a checking account, and you're writing checks. Are you sure you have enough money in your account to cover all the checks you're writing? To make sure that you do, record every check you write. Some checkbooks make carbon copies of each check you write. Most checkbooks have a separate section called a **register** in which you record the checks you write. Your check register is like a homemade bank statement!

A Balancing Act

Keeping accurate records of the checks you write is important. To make sure your records are accurate, you need to balance your checkbook monthly. This means that what your bank statement says should match your own records. Why do you think it's called balancing?

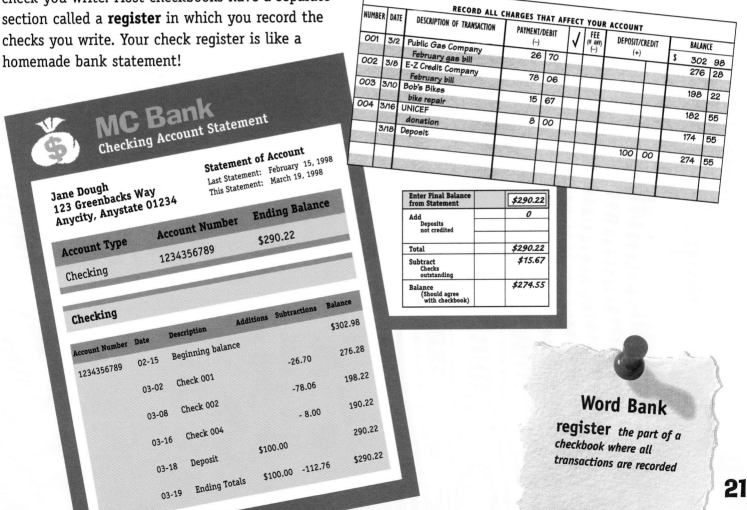

MC Bank
Checking Account Statement

Statement of Account

Jane Dough
123 Greenbacks Way
Anycity, Anystate 01234

Last Statement: February 15, 1998
This Statement: March 19, 1998

Account Type	Account Number	Ending Balance
Checking	1234356789	$290.22

Checking

Account Number	Date	Description	Additions	Subtractions	Balance
1234356789	02-15	Beginning balance			$302.98
	03-02	Check 001		-26.70	276.28
	03-08	Check 002		-78.06	198.22
	03-16	Check 004		- 8.00	190.22
	03-18	Deposit	$100.00		290.22
	03-19	Ending Totals	$100.00	-112.76	$290.22

RECORD ALL CHARGES THAT AFFECT YOUR ACCOUNT

NUMBER	DATE	DESCRIPTION OF TRANSACTION	PAYMENT/DEBIT (−)	✓	FEE (IF ANY) (−)	DEPOSIT/CREDIT (+)	BALANCE
001	3/2	Public Gas Company February gas bill	26 70				$ 302 98
002	3/8	E-Z Credit Company February bill	78 06				276 28
003	3/10	Bob's Bikes bike repair	15 67				198 22
004	3/16	UNICEF donation	8 00				182 55
	3/18	Deposit					174 55
						100 00	274 55

Enter Final Balance from Statement	$290.22
Add Deposits not credited	0
Total	$290.22
Subtract Checks outstanding	$15.67
Balance (Should agree with checkbook)	$274.55

21

The Life of a Check

Moving Right Along

Today, most money is never seen or touched. It is transferred from bank to bank electronically. This is possible because of computers. Computers speed up the way banks do business. It's a lot faster to have a computer transfer money than to carry millions of pieces of paper and coins from one bank to another—especially when some of the banks are halfway around the world! Part of this movement of money is done by checks that people write. With a check, money moves from one person to another, but no bills or coins change hands!

A Matter of Fact
If you add all of the costs of moving checks through the banking system, including the cost of paper, printing, and mailing, the total is about 80¢ per check.

1 A girl in New York buys in-line skates from the catalog of a sports store in San Francisco. Her mother mails a check to pay for them.

2 The store owner deposits the check in the store's account at its San Francisco branch.

6 The New York bank then tells its clearinghouse to subtract the amount from its account.

3 The San Francisco bank sends the check to the San Francisco **clearinghouse** that services it.

CLEARINGHOUSE

8 Finally, the San Francisco clearinghouse pays the San Francisco bank and the money goes into the store's account.

7 Now the clearinghouse that services the New York bank pays the San Francisco clearinghouse.

4 The San Francisco clearinghouse then sends the check for collection to the clearinghouse that services the New York bank that houses the account that the check was from.

CLEARINGHOUSE

5 This clearinghouse sends the check to the New York bank, which deducts the amount from the woman's account.

Word Bank
clearinghouse *a place where banks exchange checks and settle accounts*

23

Electronically

Deciphering the Check Code

Checks are processed by high-speed computers that read the instructions printed in code on the bottom of the check in special ink. This ink can be magnetized so the computer can read the code. About 2,400 checks can be sorted in one minute!

Reading a check? That doesn't sound too exciting!

I think I'll stick to reading mystery novels.

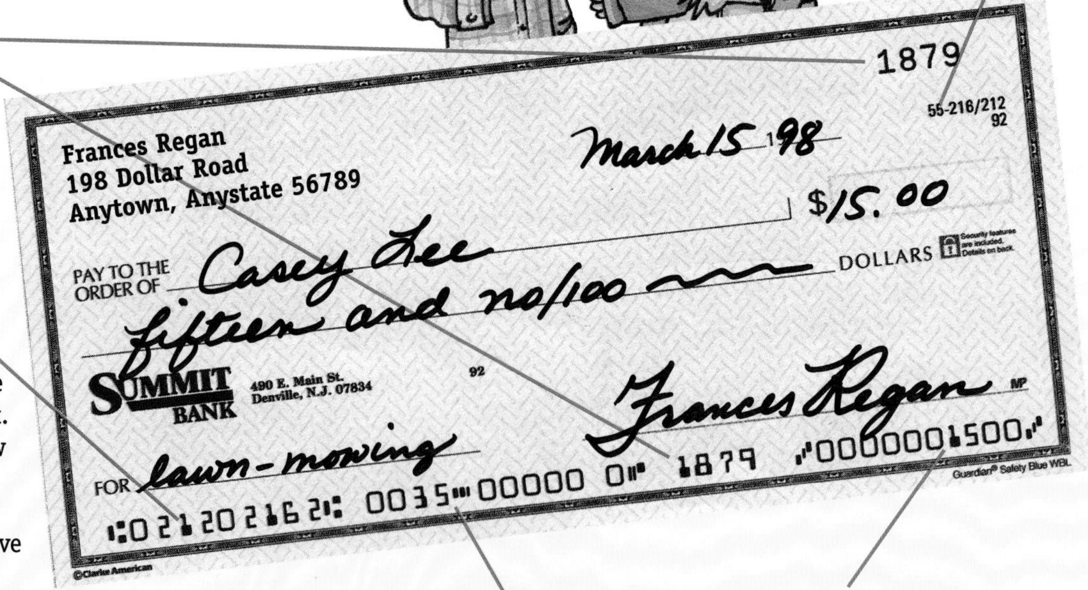

Routing number
This number is used to manually process a check.

Check number

Check-routing numbers
These numbers identify the bank that issued the check. The first two numbers show the bank's Federal Reserve district. The third number identifies the Federal Reserve branch. The fourth number shows the bank's state- or special-collection arrangement (how the money is to be collected). The last number verifies that all the previous numbers are correct.

Frances Regan
198 Dollar Road
Anytown, Anystate 56789

March 15 '98

$15.00

PAY TO THE ORDER OF Casey Lee

fifteen and no/100 ————— DOLLARS

SUMMIT BANK 490 E. Main St. Denville, N.J. 07834

FOR lawn-mowing

Frances Regan

1:0212021621: 0035 00000 0 1879 0000001500

Bank account number

Dollar amount
This amount is printed by the first bank to receive the check.

Speaking

Depositor's endorsement
In order to deposit or cash a check, you must **endorse** it, or sign your name on the back. Many banks also require customers to write their bank-account number on the check as well.

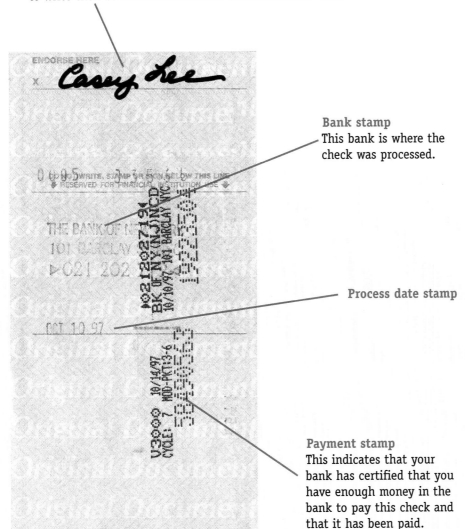

Bank stamp
This bank is where the check was processed.

Process date stamp

Payment stamp
This indicates that your bank has certified that you have enough money in the bank to pay this check and that it has been paid.

A Matter of Fact

The Federal Reserve is the government's bank, so it handles a lot of checks. If all the checks that the Federal Reserve handles in a day were laid down end to end, they would stretch from New York to Alaska!

Word Bank

endorse *to sign your name on the back of a check before depositing it*

25

Check It Out

Bounced checks and balanced checkbooks? What's next?

Checking Checks

Warning! If you write a check to your friend Mary, you must have enough money in your checking account to pay the amount on the check. If you don't have enough money, you have "insufficient funds," and the check will be returned to you. If this happens, you will have to pay a fee to the bank for this check. Some people call this kind of check a rubber check, or a **bounced check,** because it goes back to the person who wrote it. If you bounce a check and don't pay the person you gave the check to with cash or a new check, you can end up in jail.

A Matter of Fact
Almost 80% of all store sales in the United States are made to people who pay with either checks or credit cards. So, what percent of people pay with cash?

Traveling With Checks

You've probably seen ads on TV about people on vacation who lose their cash. How do you think travelers avoid this? If you said traveler's checks, you're right! For a small fee you can buy **traveler's checks** at most banks and credit unions. You can even buy the checks in a foreign currency. Traveler's checks are a safe way to carry money to places that won't accept credit cards or personal checks. Traveler's checks work just like cash. If you pay for something that costs eight dollars with a ten-dollar traveler's check, you'd get two dollars change.

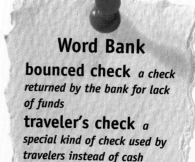

Word Bank
bounced check *a check returned by the bank for lack of funds*
traveler's check *a special kind of check used by travelers instead of cash*

It's Official!

Suppose you are an adult who wants to buy a car that costs $8,000. If you want to write a check, the car dealer may require you to have your check guaranteed by a bank. You could have the bank certify, or guarantee, one of your own checks. The bank does this only after checking the current balance of your account to make sure you have enough money to cover the check. You could also purchase a single check from the bank, called a **cashier's check**. A cashier's check is just like a certified check, except that the money comes from the bank's account after the money is transferred from your account. Either way, the car dealer has the bank's word that the check can be cashed.

Why Not Cash?

Checks are everywhere! They have become the most common medium of exchange in the U.S. People write checks more often than they use cash. Checks aren't necessarily better than cash, but in many ways they are easier. Checks are safer to send or carry than cash, because cash is more easily stolen, and a check has value only if it is signed by the owner of the checking account.

A Penny for Your Thoughts

Now that you know all about checking accounts, do you think that you would rather write a check or use a debit card? Why?

No Need for Checks?

The use of debit cards has reduced the use of checks and has also made banking cheaper. In the future you may not even need checks. You'll just call up a store and place an order for something. The store will contact your bank electronically. The bank will use its computers to automatically take money from your account and put it into the seller's account. This is called **electronic funds transfer**. In fact, we already transfer money electronically when we use an ATM or pay bills by computer. What are some advantages and disadvantages to doing business this way?

Word Bank

cashier's check *a check that you buy from a bank that is guaranteed by the bank*

electronic funds transfer *the movement of money from one account to another via computer*

27

Take Your Pick!

It's Your Money

Suppose you receive $10 allowance each week. Each week you put $4 in your savings account, $3 in your checking account, and keep $3 for spending money. How long would it take you to add $20 to your savings account?

Logical Savings

How much does each person have in his or her savings account?

It All Adds Up (or Does It?)

Suppose you deposit $100 in a bank. Each year you receive 5% interest on your $100. Each year you take out $5 for spending money. How long will it take until your balance reaches $150?

Once Upon a Time . . .

Imagine that you're a check. Tell a funny story describing your travels and adventures from the bank to someone's checkbook to a business to a clearinghouse and back to the bank. What happens to you? Whom do you meet? What kind of trouble do you get into along the way?

I have $3 more than you in my account.

I have $11 less than you in my account.

I have twice as much as you in my account.

I can't even open an account!

Chapter 3

All About
Credit

What it is,
what it's not, and
how to use it!

I wonder if I have enough credit to buy this computer.

Some people couldn't live without them. Other people refuse to use them. What are they? Credit cards!

What is credit? What's the difference between credit cards and checks?

How old do you have to be to get a credit card?

What are some advantages to using credit?

What are some disadvantages?

Take the time to find the answers to these questions and more in this chapter. When you're finished reading, give yourself some credit for learning all the facts.

It's In-credit-ible!

Talking Credit

Did you know that you can buy something without money? No, it's not free. It's **credit!** Credit means that someone is willing to lend you money and give you time to pay it back, usually for a fee or with interest. Credit lets you buy now and pay later. Consumers use credit to buy the things they need or want, such as houses, clothing, or cars. Businesses use credit to expand and grow. Even federal, state, and local governments use credit to build and repair things like roads, bridges, and schools.

LOW INTEREST

BUY NOW PAY LATER

Low Monthly Payments

Word Bank

credit *money loaned, usually for a fee, that must be repaid*

debt *money owed to a person or business*

down payment *an amount of money paid as an initial lump sum payment for a debt*

installment *partial payment of a debt, paid regularly*

line of credit *an agreed-upon amount of money that can be borrowed from a bank*

In Search of... Credit

Where can you get credit? Banks, businesses, and individuals can give credit. A friend of yours who buys you a snack and lets you pay him or her back later is giving you credit. He or she trusts you to pay the money back.

Some stores will allow you to buy very expensive items on credit. However, you might have to pay a certain portion of the **debt**, or the money you owe, as a **down payment**. You pay the balance, or the rest of the bill, in small amounts each month, called **installments**, plus interest. So the item actually costs more than its original price. What's the point, you ask? You can get what you need or want now, even if you don't have the money to pay with cash.

Banking on Credit

Banks give credit to their customers in lots of ways, such as mortgages, installment loans, credit cards, and **lines of credit**. A line of credit means that a prearranged amount of money is available for you in the bank whenever you need to use it. Any money you borrow, you must repay, with interest. But if you don't borrow any money, you pay nothing. For instance, if you have a $5,000 line of credit and you only use $1,000, you will only have to pay back $1,000, plus any interest. On the other hand, with mortgages and loans, you get all of the money at one time upfront.

30

Checking
You Out

Will a bank give credit to anyone who asks for it? No. State laws vary, but you usually have to be 18 or 21 to apply for credit. Also, a bank will only give credit to someone it feels sure will pay back the loan. What are some ways banks know you'll pay them back? One way banks do this is to run a credit check on you to make sure you pay your bills on time. If you've never borrowed from a bank before, you may also need **collateral** for your loan. Collateral is something valuable, like jewelry, stocks, or bonds, that you give to the bank to hold until the loan is paid off. If you **default**, or don't repay the loan, the bank can sell the collateral. You may also be required to have someone, such as a parent with a good credit history, **cosign** the loan. This means that your parent is responsible for repaying the loan if you can't.

A Matter of Fact

The word *credit* comes from the Latin word *creditus*, meaning "to trust." When someone lends you money, he or she is trusting you to repay it.

Shopping Around

What's the most important thing you do before you make a major purchase? Why, shop around! That way you're sure you're paying the best price. When you need credit, the same rule applies. Shop around. Check what different banks charge. Find the different conditions, or **credit terms**, for the credit that you want.

Some banks charge customers to apply for credit. Other banks offer lower interest rates but charge a fee if your payment is late. Interest rates and loan terms may also vary among banks. Remember, there is always a trade-off between the amount of time you take to repay money, and the amount of money you pay each month. If you can only afford a small monthly payment, it will take you longer to repay your debt. The longer you take to repay, the more interest you'll pay to the bank.

Word Bank

collateral *property, such as a house or car, that a borrower promises to give to a lender in case of a loan default*

default *to fail to repay a loan*

cosign *to sign a document for another person, indicating responsibility if the borrower defaults*

credit terms *conditions of credit, such as interest rates and fees*

What a **Card!**

What's plastic, flat, about the size of a playing card, and can be used like money? If you answered "a credit card," you're right! Millions of Americans have **credit cards**. Credit cards are used to pay for vacations, clothing, books, computers, groceries, and even taxes! You can buy goods and services wherever your card is accepted and pay for them later. What a deal! Or is it?

There are strings attached to credit cards. Unless you pay the full amount you owe each month, the goods or services you buy with the credit card end up being more expensive than if you had paid for them with cash or a check. This happens because interest is added to the cost of your purchase. So a credit card should be used very carefully!

Where Do I **Get** One?

Banks are the main sources of credit cards. Bank-issued credit cards can be used at any business that accepts them. Many stores and service companies also issue credit cards. These cards can only be used at the store or company that issued them. But they work just the same as bank credit cards. People often have several credit cards: one or two from banks, and others from stores and companies they use often.

Wow! I only have to pay $2 a month for all these biscuits!

At that rate it will take 20 years to pay off the bill.

You'd better eat slowly!

Walter Cavanagh

A Matter of Fact
The Guinness Book of World Records reports that Walter Cavanagh of Santa Clara, California, owns the largest number of credit cards. "Mr. Plastic Fantastic," as he likes to be called, has 1,356 different cards! He keeps them in the world's longest wallet—250 feet long and weighing 37½ pounds!

Word Bank

credit card *a card that allows a person to make purchases on credit*

32

Credit

Why Do They Do It?

Why do banks and companies provide people with credit cards? Because they make money from them! Every month the bank sends cardholders a bill showing everything they bought with the card that month. Some banks allow cardholders to pay just part of the bill each month. If a cardholder chooses to pay part of the bill, he or she must pay interest to the bank on the amount of money that is still owed, plus interest on any new charges. Some cards don't charge interest at all. But you have to pay a membership fee each year, called an annual fee, and you have to pay the balance due each month on your bill.

It's in the Cards

How do the stores that accept bank credit cards get paid? After you make a purchase with your credit card, the store where you made the purchase contacts the bank that issued your credit card. The bank then pays the store for everything that is charged on the card. The bank also charges the store a fee for this service. The bank then bills you for the amount of the purchase. The bank pays the store, and you pay the bank.

Bonus!

Some credit card companies give you bonuses for using their card. Some let you earn "miles" for every dollar you charge on your card, which you can turn in to receive free plane tickets. Other companies donate money to charity whenever you charge something on your card. Some companies even give you consumer protection with any item you buy with your card. That means if you lose or break the item within a certain amount of time after you bought it, the credit card company will replace it for free! Or will it be free? Where does the credit card company get the money to replace the item? From the interest and fees it charges its customers—including you!

A Penny for Your Thoughts

Why are stores willing to pay the bank a fee to allow customers to use a credit card? What benefits does the store get? Do you think these benefits are worth it?

Payback Time

Remember bank statements? If you have a credit card, you also receive a monthly statement from the credit card company. Take a look at the credit card statement below.

Payment due
This is the date when you must make your next payment.

Previous balance
This is how much you owed last month.

Account This number is used by the bank to identify your account.

Payments, credits
This is how much you paid last month and how much money was credited to your account. If you didn't pay the whole balance, you will pay interest on the money you owe.

E-Z Credit Company

Statement Date: 4/15
Payment Due: 5/07

Account: 55512123434
Credit Limit: $500

Credit limit
This is the limit on the total amount of money you can charge.

	TOTAL
Previous Balance	$25.00
(-) Payments/Credits	25.00
(+) Purchases	66.75
(-) Finance Charges	0.00
(=) New Balance	66.75
Minimum Payment	$10.00

Purchases This is how much you charged on your card this month.

New balance This is how much you owe now.

Date	Transactions	Credits	Charges
		$25.00	
3/21	Payment		$45.25
3/26	X-Pressly for You Shop		$6.00
3/26	Pizza Plus		$15.50
4/06	Music Maniac		
Total of Credits and Charges		$25.00	$66.75

Charges
This is a detailed description of all of your purchases from the past month.

Minimum payment
This is the least amount of money you must pay this month.

34

Word Bank
credit limit *the amount of credit available to a person*

Cards or Checks?

When you use a credit card, you're really taking out a loan from a bank or a credit card company. The bank or company pays the store and then bills you for the money you charged to the credit card. If you pay by check, the money comes directly from your checking account. If you don't have the money, you can't make the purchase. But you pay a price for using the credit card—it's called interest!

Pay now?

Pay later?

Either way you have to pay.

A Matter of Fact
Americans have more than 500 million credit cards. More than half of those cards are VISA cards.

What's in Store for You?

What's the best way for you to get credit for the first time? Be responsible! You need to show the bank or credit card company that you're able to handle money. One way to show you are credit worthy is to get and keep a job. That way, the credit card company knows that you have a regular income available to pay your credit card bills. Another way to do this is to open a savings account and deposit money regularly. Then when you want to apply for credit, the savings account will show that you are a consistent customer. Paying bills on time is also important.

The easiest kind of credit to get for the first time is a department store credit card. Many stores have special charge accounts for teenagers. To open this kind of account, a parent or other adult must usually cosign. If you are old enough, the customer service department will give you an application to fill out.

So far, so good, but now to the most important part of a department store credit card application: the *Retail Installment Credit Agreement*. This agreement lets you know the terms of the credit agreement. It tells you whether you must pay your bill all at once or if you can pay in installments. The interest rate you'll be charged if you don't pay the whole bill is also explained. Now that you understand all this, you just need to wait for approval.

It Isn't Only Plastic

Credit—
Good Idea or Bad?

Credit cards make buying very easy. But a credit card is not a license to spend money. You should be careful not to charge more than you are able to pay. Credit cards themselves are also an expense. As you learned before, many cards charge a yearly fee. The interest rates for credit cards are usually much higher than the interest rates on bank loans. An unpaid credit card balance can build up interest pretty quickly. Here are some tips for being a wise credit user.

- Understand the terms of your credit agreement. Read it carefully. Find out exactly how much money you have to pay each month. Usually, the greater the amount that you charge, the more you have to pay.

- Save all the sales receipts from purchases you make on credit. Then you will have a record of how much money you have spent each month. You will also have a record in case the store makes a mistake with your bill.

- Don't use your credit card for every purchase. Pay cash when you can. Paying cash is always cheaper.

- Plan your purchases. If you know you need to buy several expensive items, try to spread out your buying over time. That way you won't have to pay a large credit card bill.

- Choose a few credit cards that you know you will use. It will be easier to keep track of your money, and you won't be paying lots of interest and annual fees.

A Matter of Fact

Can you imagine a credit card that thinks? One such "smart card" is being used in France today. These credit cards come with built-in computers that record each transaction made with the card. That makes record-keeping a whole lot easier!

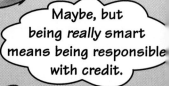

I'm smarter than these guys.

Maybe, but being really smart means being responsible with credit.

Don't Shop for Trouble

You've just received your credit card statement, and there's a charge on it for 15 pairs of basketball sneakers! And you don't even *like* basketball! Someone must have used your credit card, and now you have an enormous bill. What do you do? Under federal law, you are only required to pay $50 if your card is stolen and used by someone else. But if you lose your card or think it's been stolen, you must call the credit card company right away. They will cancel your card and give you a new one. Hopefully, they will catch the person who is going on an illegal shopping spree.

Do you know someone who has bought something over the phone or through a computer? You can pay for such a purchase with a credit card, but you must be careful. Other people can use your number to charge things, even without having your card. So, if you find an unexpected purchase on your monthly statement, be sure to call your credit card company right away.

It's Your Turn to Take the Credit

Every day you make decisions about money. Whether you're shopping for a computer or a pair of shoes, there are always things to consider. How much am I prepared to spend? Which is the best buy? Do I really need this? Do I need it *now*? Should I buy on credit, or wait until I have the cash and save money? There's a lot to think about.

Credit cards make buying things easy—sometimes too easy. You have to stay on your toes and be a smart "charger" as well as a smart shopper. You have to manage your own money—and your credit—and that takes a lot of planning. As you can see, there's a lot more to money than just dollars and cents!

A Penny for Your Thoughts

It used to be a custom in America for engaged couples to exchange coins as pledges of love. Do you think the idea of exchanging credit cards will ever catch on? Why or why not?

CREDIT CARD STATEMENT

SNEAKER	$	1,500
HEAVEN		
15 PAIR		
@ $100⁰⁰ EA		
	$	1,500

37

Take Your Pick!

Extra Charge!

Many different businesses now offer credit cards. Phone companies, charitable organizations, and even baseball teams offer them. When you make purchases using these cards, you may receive benefits, like free phone calls, or money may be donated to a charitable organization. Which bonus would you like to get from a credit card?

Credit: Pro or Con?

In the chart are reasons why people like *and* dislike credit. But they're all mixed up. Decide which ones are advantages to having credit and which ones are disadvantages.

yearly fees

protection from theft

spending what you can't afford

accepted all over the world

good for emergencies

interest payments

Have a Bite!

Chez Chucky Menu

apple juice	small	$1.00
	large	$1.50
lemonade	small	$ .75
	large	$1.00
hamburger		$2.00
tuna		$2.50
fruit salad		$1.50
yogurt		$1.75

Charge your lunch on a credit card! What would you order for lunch from Chez Chucky? How much would it cost? Don't forget to add the tax and tip!

38

Glossary

ATM card a bank card that allows customers to use an ATM machine

automated-teller machine (ATM) a machine that performs most of the banking operations that a human teller can

balance the amount of money in a bank account

bank a business that keeps money for customers, makes loans, and provides other money-related services

bank statement a monthly summary of a customer's bank transactions

bounced check a check returned by the bank for lack of funds

cash bills and coins, or to give or get cash for, as in to *cash* a check

cashier's check a check guaranteed by the bank

check a written order to a bank to pay a specified amount of money to a specified person or company, from money on deposit with the bank

circulation money that is available for use

clearinghouse a place where banks exchange checks and settle accounts

collateral property, such as a house or car, that a borrower promises to give to a lender in case of a loan default

cosign to sign a document for another person, indicating responsibility if the borrower defaults

credit money loaned, usually for a fee, that must be repaid

credit card a card that allows a person to make purchases on credit

credit limit the amount of credit available to a person

credit terms conditions of credit, such as interest rates and fees

debit card a bank card that allows a person to withdraw money electronically from a checking account

debt money owed to a person or business

default to fail to repay a loan

deposit the money put in a bank account

direct deposit electronic deposit of checks in a bank

down payment an amount of money paid as an initial lump sum payment for a debt

electronic funds transfer the movement of money from one account to another via computer

endorse to sign your name on the back of a check

Federal Reserve the central bank of the United States

fee money charged for a service

installment partial payment of a debt, paid regularly

interest the money a person pays to borrow money, or the money a bank pays depositors for using their money

line of credit an agreed-upon amount of money that can be borrowed from a bank

loan a sum of money borrowed for a certain amount of time

minimum balance a fixed amount of money required in a customer's account to avoid paying bank fees

minimum deposit the least amount of money required to open an account

money order a written order, or check, that a certain sum of money be paid to a certain person or business

mortgage a loan given to pay for a house or building

pawnbroker a person who lends money at a specified interest rate to people who leave items as security

pawnshop a place to leave an item of value in exchange for a loan

PC banking using a home or office computer to carry out bank transactions

personal identification number (PIN) a code that activates an ATM card

principal a sum of money in an account, not including interest

profit the money a business makes after expenses are paid

register the part of a checkbook where transactions are recorded

retirement when a person gives up his or her job, often because of age

safe-deposit box a place to keep special items at a bank

savings money that is put away to be used later

transaction any business done with the bank, such as a deposit or withdrawal

traveler's check a special kind of check used by travelers instead of cash

withdrawal the removal of money from a bank account

Index

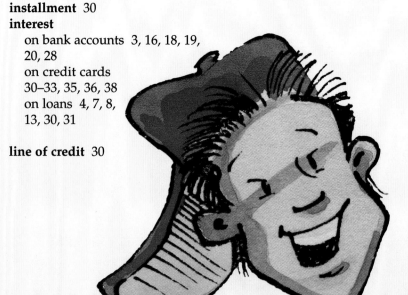